11 ½ Ways to Ignite Your Creativity

Dennis Russell Hodges

Kansas City   Spartan Press   Missouri

Spartan Press
Kansas City, MO
spartanpresskc@gmail.com

Spartan
Press

Copyright © Dennis Hodges, 2018

First Edition 1 3 5 7 9 10 8 6 4 2

ISBN: 978-1-946642-50-9

LCCN: 2018940724

Design, edits and layout: Jason Ryberg,

Cover design: Scott Gross (144design.co)

Author photo: Judit Hodges

Acknowledgements

Foreword / 1

Chapter 1 - Reboot Your Mornings / 5

Chapter 2 - Alter Your Routine / 12

Chapter 3 - Turn Off the Devices / 18

Chapter 4 - Monotask / 25

Chapter 5 - Go Analog / 31

Chapter 6 - Actively Engage Your Senses / 36

Chapter 7 - Go Live / 43

Chapter 8 - Take a Workshop / 48

Chapter 9 - Get the Tools / 53

Chapter 10 - Take Time Off / 60

Chapter 11 - Travel Somewhere / 65

Chapter 12 - The ½ Idea / 71

Afterword / 77

About the Author / 79

Writing a book is more than a solitary endeavor.
I would like to thank those who helped me bring this
together: Rick Kemmis, for being my "accountabuddy",
helping me stay focused and on task. Scott Gross of
144design.co for his amazing talent as demonstrated by
the book cover design. Brad Anderson for making
connections and challenging me. The essential proofreaders,
each of whom found mistakes and offered suggestions to
improve passages: Tony Wawryk, Peggy Wagoner,
Bob Block, Dianne Smith, Nancy Liston, Stacie Danks,
Lee Shiney, David Lake and Janis Angermayr.

To my wife, Judit, whose belief, encouragement and patience can be summarized in one word: love.

Foreword

It's simple, really: I believe that everyone is creative. Do you feel you are creative? If you answered "no" think back to when you were five years old. Were you creative then? Exactly. If you answered "yes", then good answer!

Regardless of how you responded, you are looking for inspiration to, obviously, ignite your creativity. Let's see if we can make that happen, shall we?

First, a quick technical dive to set the stage. If you know me, you know that the words "Dennis" and "technical" are never used in the same sentence, so don't worry that you're going to glaze over while I dive into the weeds. Ignite, by definition,[1] is "to catch fire or cause to catch fire." Often, what ignites something is a spark. A spark is a catalyst — it does not change its form, but it causes change in that with which it interacts. This book is a catalyst; it is that spark.

Everyone I know, including myself, has so much going on in their lives. We all live a complicated existence! My life began to get complicated when, as a teenager, I had more than one key on my keychain. Life has not become less complicated since then.

Rather, life is as complicated today as it has ever been in the history of humans. With our connected devices — believe me, I can't imagine living without them — it is so easy to be caught up in the flood of life: to always be plugged in and going, going, going all of the time with literally no time for ourselves. No time to just pause and think.

No time to literally or figuratively stop and smell the roses. It's no surprise that many people feel they are less creative than they'd like to be. Creativity takes even just a little amount of time and none of us seem to have spare time.

I'm no different from you. Yes, I see myself as a creative person, but as I stated at the beginning, this falls in the category of what makes us human. With all of the normal daily pressures, it's easy to lose touch with this essential characteristic of ourselves. It happens without even thinking about it. As time goes by — days, months, even years — our creativity gets buried in the noise that surrounds us. We need is a personal reset button to clear the clutter. Maybe this is that reset.

This book is based on personal experience and proven techniques. I've shared these with others who've found they work for them, too. So, here they are conveniently summarized. You'll find that some of them are "quick wins" — things you can do now and see immediate effect — while others will take a little more effort and planning. Regardless, none of them require a Ph.D. or a gazillion dollars to put into action. I like to keep things simple and helpful.

To help you absorb the concepts shared here, try three things: one is to play music while you read the book. There is evidence[2] that listening to music while you read helps with comprehension, although not all music is created equal for this task. Give it a try and see if it helps you. Second, carve out some time with this book.

Time to focus on just the concepts shared here. Third, make a cup of tea or coffee or pour a glass of wine and enjoy the moment while you dive in.

Also note that each chapter has a place where you can jot some notes to yourself. Just another way to help the ideas sink in.

Albert Schweitzer[3] said, "Sometimes our light goes out but is blown into flame by another human being." I'm not sure your light has gone out, but I do hope these 11 ½ ideas fan your flame and ignite your creativity.

Time to light up things. Ready?

Dennis Hodges
March, 2018

Chapter 1
Reboot Your Mornings

Think about what happens when you wake up on a typical morning. What is the exact sequence of things that you do? Jot them down on this list, starting with how you wake up through the first ten things you do. Don't leave any steps out, as small as they may seem.

My Typical Morning

1. get out of bed
2. turn off alarm
3. go to the bathroom
4. take out retainers
5. get dressed
6. do my hair
7. mascara
8. take vitamins
9. drink water
10. eat

In that first ten steps list, did you list "check social media or email"? Was it near the top of the list, perhaps just after "turn off alarm"? Raise your hand if you are guilty as charged. Based on asking this question at my keynotes and workshops, I'd say there was a 60-70% chance you raised your hand.

Think about what the above sequence does for a moment. You've just awakened from (hopefully) a good night's rest. Your body and mind are recharged, refreshed. You've just left that dream state where ideas often finally emerge or you have the solution to that challenge that's been dogging you or you finally remember the name that you couldn't recall yesterday. When you open your phone and reconnect with the world outside of your home, all of those great thoughts vaporize. Suddenly, you are drawn back into the real world, and even into work — and you're still in bed! Why do we do this to ourselves?

You see, all the cool things going on in your head when you first awaken are a result of your brain having time to sort through the data it amassed during the previous day. I view the brain as an office full of cubicles. As each cubicle has a specific function to perform, so do the areas and nodes of your brain. Yes, they work together on certain tasks, but they each have their own "to-do" list for which they are primarily responsible. When we sleep, I envision the workers in this cubicle farm coming out to have beers with their colleagues, like an after-work mixer. Colleagues have a chance to relax and catch up with one another in a non-stressful environment. The workday is done and it's time to relax. Business still gets discussed, albeit informally. That's when the connections happen in our brains: when we're relaxed.

When you are awake there are so many stimuli coming at you, it's hard enough to stay on top of the top-of-mind issues on which you are working. At night — your mind's happy hour — your brain sorts through things in your subconscious and makes the connections you could not while you were awake. I'm no neurologist as you've already figured out, so please don't hold me to technical and medical descriptions.

After sleeping, you wake up refreshed because, first, your body had a much-needed rest and second, your conscious mind also had its rest.

When you check your phone first thing you are immediately back in the real world with all of its noises and pressures. If you checked your email, you are also back at work — and you're still in your jammies! That is so unfair! You're lying there in your favorite cartoon character pajamas (come on, admit you have them) and, because you are starting to get ready for the day and you are reading, (maybe even answering) emails, you are also multitasking!

What would happen if you didn't check your emails / social media / news / whatever first thing? What would happen if you let it all sit there for a while — say, an hour? Would your world come to an end? I rather doubt it. Would you be so far behind that you could never catch up if it all waits just a few minutes more? Also doubtful.

How different would the start of your day be if you let your phone just sit there while you hop into the shower and continue enjoying that early morning refresh moment?

Wouldn't that be sublime? Delay the pressures
of the day for just a few minutes more?

If you think about it, it wasn't that long ago when we
didn't carry every aspect of our lives with us, in our
pockets, 24/7. Mornings started without the intrusion
from the outside world; without us knowing every little
thing about our friends and acquaintances first thing or
without us being dragged into the office from our bedside.
Those days are behind us and indeed it's certainly convenient
to have data literally at our fingertips, but we need to find a
way to manage this access. This is one simple step in that
direction.

Can the real world wait for a little while? Really ask yourself that question, please, as it can make all the difference in
your life.

I try to wait an hour before I check what's going on in the
world and even longer before I check emails. All of that can
wait — at least long enough for me to take a few minutes for
myself and set the tone of the day on my terms.

There's also a growing body of evidence[4] that suggests we
are at our creative peak first thing in the morning. What I've
shared earlier is a large part of the reason we have great
ideas when we first open our eyes.

What if you took this reboot of your morning to the
extreme? What if you not only kept the real world at bay
for just a little while but also took advantage of that early
morning creativity peak?

A way to test if this creative break works for you is simple: try taking a few minutes with pencil and paper to just jot the thoughts that come into your head. That's it. Or try writing in a journal, perhaps capturing three things for which you are grateful. How would that affect the start of your day and your personal creativity? It's a rather subtle change, but it is a significant one. Setting the tone for how you start your day on your terms is a fairly easy — and genuinely important — way to spark your creativity.

Try rebooting your mornings. Leave the real world "out there" for some amount of time. Take a few minutes just for yourself when you first wake up and capture those amazing thoughts fresh in your mind. Try writing down whatever comes to mind first thing in the morning.

You'll be amazed at the ideas you come up with and you'll quickly see how this one small shift in your day will have a major impact on your perspective, your stress and your creativity.

Ideas and Inspiration:

Chapter 2
Alter Your Routine

We are creatures of habit. Habits, structures and routines help us compartmentalize and organize our lives. They also blind us to what's around us.

Try this: step outside your home — use the door you usually enter from — and then step back in. When you re-enter your home, purposefully look around for things that are, to someone who's never seen your place before, out of place. Maybe it's a pair of shoes always by the door, but they really don't belong there. Or it's a stack of mail that really should be stored in a different place. Perhaps it's a decorative item that was set down once and just stayed, but it really belongs somewhere else. Whatever it is, I'm pretty certain you have something in your home that is, by most definitions, out of place, but you don't see it.

This is a product of what's known as "inattentional blindness", a term coined by Arien Mack and Irvin Rock.[5] The concept is that you don't see what's right before your eyes because you are focused on something else. That is how the item that's out of place in your home gets missed. It's been there long enough that you have essentially become blind to it. Only by deliberately looking at it and considering whether it belongs there do you see it.

The same concept is true in your everyday life. Consider your commute to work. Most likely you go the same way every day. You rarely change this and you're not alone; it's a normal part of how we manage ourselves. Routines and patterns give us predictability and help us balance the out-of-control aspects of our lives. You know your commute is more or less X minutes to and from your home. The exception to this known time is when something out of the ordinary happens — a road closure, an accident, bad weather — occurrences which are out of your control that change your otherwise predictable experience.

Edward de Bono suggests these incidents that alter your routine have a positive affect on creativity. de Bono talks about being "blocked by openness:[6]" that without obstacles that alter our routine, we don't see the possibilities. If you drive to work unobstructed, without congestion, you do not see things differently. Toss in a roadblock or traffic jam that requires you to detour and to take a new route and you'll break through those established patterns. Our brains, he argues, follow established patterns which, in turn, make living easier. Fewer decisions or choices mean less variety and a simpler existence. Less variety and a simpler existence also equals missing the possibilities.

The good news is that it doesn't have to be this way! By consciously making choices to mix things up, we can exercise our non-linear thinking and literally see our world differently. It is easier said than done; it's simply easier for us to follow the established patterns in our brains. In other words, stick to our routines.

So, what does this have to do with igniting creativity?

Go back to entering your home and looking at it with purpose. What else is there you miss because it's always been like that? Alternatively, consider what hasn't changed significantly in a number of years, like furniture that's in the same place or walls that are the same color they've always been, etc. Try applying, to your own world, what's known as the "Hawthorne effect."[7] This concept is based on studies in the early 1900s at a factory outside of Chicago where, by making changes to the work environment — increasing the brightness of the light, relocating work-stations, and even cleaning up work areas — employees showed an increase in productivity.

If you were to make changes in your home — put that thing away that doesn't belong where it's been sitting, rearrange furniture, change the lighting, repaint certain walls — what influence could these have on your outlook? Your energy? Your creativity?

Or take a simpler creative look at your home. For example, look for how sunlight comes in through windows and doors. What patterns of light and shadow are there that you normally miss? What compositions are created by light and shadow and how do they change throughout the day and seasons?

As you head to work, try looking at sights along the normal route of your commute; really look at the things you pass and try to see them anew. By purposefully looking at the world around you, you will see some amazing things — odd juxtapositions, interesting patterns, things that are simply accepted as "that's how they've always been", even if they may not make sense. A building painted an awful color. Cool street art. A makeshift shelter for the homeless. A business you've never entered (and perhaps should even just to learn what's there).

As you enter your workspace, look at it with the same critical eye as you did your home. *Really* look at it for opportunities to make changes. Regardless of where you work and what job you do, what changes can you make to that space — similar to what you did at home — that will alter your patterns and help you see your work in, perhaps literally, a new light?

Change doesn't come easily. It takes effort. We — all of us — are comfortable with our established patterns, our routines, and accepting how things are. Face it, it's easy and requires little to no thought.

Try this:

Close Your Eyes.

Close your eyes and imagine yourself walking in the front door of your home. Can you, in your mind's eye, "walk" through your home and identify where each and every piece of furniture is? My guess is you can and come pretty close to getting most of it right. You can probably nail your workspace as well, since it's most likely a smaller space and because you spend so many of your waking hours there.

Try the same experiment with your commute to work. In this case, there will be a lot less detail — you will be able to identify larger landmarks and significant details (specific turns, traffic lights, street names, certain buildings) but a lot of the detail will be less clear. This is the result of inattentional blindness combined with being blocked by openness. You simply miss a lot of the subtle nuances unless you challenge yourself to literally see them.

Changing your routine or physical world isn't necessarily easy. We like our routines. We like that we can navigate our homes in complete darkness without banging our shins or stubbing our toes on furniture. We like not having to think or challenge ourselves unnecessarily, particularly when it comes to the mundane, predictable and repetitive aspects of our lives.

Shifting your way of thinking is paradoxical: the more you push yourself, altering your route or changing routines, the more comfortable you become with the uncertainties these changes present. Purposefully seeing the world around you or altering your daily habits are great ways to ignite your creativity.

Ideas and Inspiration:

Chapter 3
Turn Off the Devices

Are you a digital native or a digital immigrant? I ask because it may influence how you read this chapter.

I am a digital immigrant. I remember the days before the internet. Before mobile phones. Before the desktop PC. Before the fax. Before FedEx. I have not, however, ever sent a telegram or a letter by Pony Express, just so you know I don't go back *that* far.

A digital native on the other hand, is someone who does not remember a time in his or her life without ubiquitous connectivity. As far as a native knows, we've always had this connectivity and these devices. At a minimum, a digital native does not remember time before the Internet.

This distinction is significant. Someone who lived in The Time Before Devices should remember (although it's hard sometimes) how life was when there were no devices. When you left work, you left work. If you missed a program on television, it was gone. If someone called you on your home telephone after 9:00 PM it must be an emergency. There were times when your life was just quiet, giving you time to get lost in your thoughts without distractions.

For a digital native, this constant connectivity is a natural part of life and you simply do not know anything different. Being in touch with everyone and everything at any time is normal and expected. You can be contacted wherever you are, for whatever reason, whenever someone wants to contact you, is how it's always been. The concept of what constitutes quiet time is abstract in comparison to the generations that came before you.

Today, this constant connectivity touches young and old alike. We're all plugged in to the point that we're nearly unaware of just how connected we really are.

Starting with checking our phones first thing in the morning (and you've committed to stop doing this starting tomorrow, right?!) we are in front of a screen of some kind nearly 12 hours a day. Do the math: 24 hours in the day (regardless of where you live on this marbled bowling ball we call home), 12 hours in front of a screen, and 6-8 hours of sleep (I may be optimistic or idealistic here, but work with me). Add those up and we are left with 4-6 hours a day for everything else in our lives. Eating, commuting, time with family, time alone, shopping — everything else that comprises our daily schedules has to be packed into those few hours a day. Crazy.

So, what to do?

How about just turning off the devices? Now that you've picked yourself up off the floor from laughter, think about it: if you spend less time in front of one of the many screens in your life, how might you use that time?

What could you do with that newfound time in your day? How could you use it to move forward creatively?

Aside from disbelief that I would even suggest turning off your device(s), you may want to ask me, "OK, if I do turn mine off or even just walk away from it for a while, how long are you thinking?" Fair question. How much time do you think you'd need to see an impact on your creativity?

Would you believe 10 minutes a day?

That's it; just 10 minutes. A day. Sounds crazy, no? Doesn't sound like enough time to do anything productive or creative does it? Why, 10 minutes is hardly any time at all! 10 minutes flies by in the blink of an eye! It couldn't possibly have a positive impact on one's creativity. But it can.

Here's the backstory: I've already come clean, admitting that I used to check my phone first thing in the morning. When I rebooted my days, one thing I did was grab a pencil and paper and sit and write whatever came to mind. (I've mentioned this already and will go more into this technique later.)

What's key is that I didn't take a long time to write; I told myself to take a minimum of 10 minutes to write and then get going with my day. As the experiment unfolded, I started taking multiple (two to three) 10-minute pauses a day. Not every day, but most days. Just 10 minutes away from distractions, in particular my phone, computer, and tablet.

What I haven't shared with you yet is that, at that time, I had a corner of my desk where my personal creative projects went to die. Or at least slumber for a very long time to the point that they might as well be dead. I'd have this great idea, jot it down on either a piece of paper or type it into a document on my computer, print it out and place it on the pile to work on later.

Except that date never came. The pile just grew larger and dustier and a huge number of cool creative projects didn't go anywhere. I never realized them; other things just got in the way.

Once I started taking my 10-minute pauses, the glacier began to move. In just a few weeks, I began to see my seeds of ideas sprout, start to take shape, and move forward. I felt so energized that momentum began to build and, through a series of these simple, short breaks, my projects became more than brain farts. They actually began to live! I can't say it was deliberate; it just happened that often during my 10-minute pauses I would think about those abandoned projects. As a result they began to get the attention they deserved and, consequently, came to life.

"Nice story," you say. "But I'm different." True, perhaps.

Realizing I was a research sample size of one, I grew curious — if this technique worked for me, could it work for others as well? To find out, I hired Millward Brown, the research company, to do a global study[8] of working adults age 18+ to test the concept. The participants agreed to take at least one 10-minute break a day away from devices, armed with nothing more than a pencil and paper, and write whatever came to mind. The test period was 30 days, as it takes at least 20 days for a change in your life to become a normal part of it, a habit if you will. We did pre-and post-tests with the participants to track their attitudes. Here's the scoop on what we learned:

Within just 30 days of taking at least one 10-minute break a day as requested, the participants felt more satisfied with life, more motivated, and — here it is — more creative! Each of these areas had a minimum of a 15-point increase from the start to the finish of the test.

Just from taking 10 minutes a day away from their devices. Pretty impressive.

Our devices have become so much a natural part of our lives that we often don't realize the control they have over our actions. They are like another appendage permanently attached to our bodies. Look, they are not going away, not until we can plug a chip into our brains or some other technological evolution that connects us on yet another level to the world around us. Nor do we necessarily want them to go away (although on particularly frustrating days when nothing is working as it should, I do somewhat envy the Luddites[9]).

What we can do, though, is learn to set down our devices from time to time to give us some space to be by ourselves without distractions. That's what the test was about; how might time away from devices positively influence our lives, even if it's just for a few minutes a day? You've seen the results from the research, beyond my testimonial.

Convinced yet?

Ideas and Inspiration:

Chapter 4
Monotask

You are, of course, familiar with the term "multitasking". In fact, I'd venture to guess that you *think* you do it almost every day in one form or another. You might even be doing it as you read this. Am I right?

The action is actually not multitasking, but rather it is "rapid toggling between tasks". True multitasking takes its form when, for example, a guitarist is also singing. Or an organist is using both hands and both feet to play a song on three different keyboards simultaneously. Or a drummer, like the organist, using both pairs of hands and feet to create music on multiple percussion instruments at the same time.

For the rest of us, we are simply toggling between tasks. Think about it: you're working on a document when an alert comes in that you have a new email. You open the email to give it a quick look, answer it, and then go back to the document you were working on. The steps that take place in this scenario include: You switch off from the document and switch on to read the email, shifting your thinking to what the email says while putting the document's focus on hold.

When you leave the email, you switch it off and switch the document back on, reminding yourself, however quickly, where you left off.

Switch off. Switch on. Switch off. Switch on. And on. And on.

For ease of conversation, let's call the process multitasking here. In short, it is distracting — and I only suggested two variables above. I didn't even mention notices from social media popping up or a text message or a phone call or someone walking into your office or any of the many, many other distractions that are a normal part of life and which take your attention away from on what you were trying to focus.

Each of these distractions require you to switch between tasks in order to address each of them while you are trying to move the initial project you were focused on forward toward completion. With each distraction comes a set of switches — off and on repeatedly — that interrupt your concentration and line of thinking.

One study[10] found multitasking more than 10 times a day can cost a person up to 10 points of IQ. I don't know about you, but I don't have that much to lose! And only 10 times a day of switching on and off between tasks? I think 10 switches an hour is not unusual.

A string of multitasking activities and interruptions often leads to frustration. Constantly changing directions can leave you with the feeling you will never get the initial project completed because your attention keeps getting drawn away for other priorities. Sound familiar?

What if it could be different? What if there was another solution that would help you?

Here's the big idea: to help reduce stress in your life, increase your sense of accomplishment and — get ready for it — boost your creativity, try "monotasking". Monotasking is just as it sounds: focusing on one thing for an extended period of time. Focusing on something uninterrupted to give you time to develop, explore, lose yourself in it and, depending on the complexity, even complete it or at least complete one section of it. Take the time to focus on one and only one thing. Block out the distractions to enable you to concentrate on one task and see it through to completion.

When I sat down to create this book, I was totally focused on just the book each and every time I wrote a passage. I turned off all distractions — my phone was set on silent, email alerts were disabled, no interruptions were allowed — and gave myself time to collect my thoughts and put them down on paper. I focused only on the book when I was working on the book.

In this case, I set a goal for each time when I wrote. Other tasks were calling me, needing my attention. Yet, in order to get this book completed, I needed to focus when I was writing. My monotask goal varied: sometimes I had a set amount of time I wanted to devote to writing. Other times it was a certain number of words I wanted to get down before I moved on to something new. Or it was a specific thought — think of it as a writing a chapter — of which I wanted to complete a draft while it was fresh in my mind.

Regardless, I had a clear objective and allowed myself the time necessary to focus on just that one task.

Monotasking has multiple benefits. First, it's a great way to get stuff done. When you take the time to focus on one thing, it gets accomplished. Go figure! It's also a great way to give you that sense of accomplishment because something you were working on, something that needed to be completed, is done. Contrast these benefits with multitasking — how constant distractions and interruptions compete for your attention resulting in nothing receiving the attention it deserves and you end up distracted, tired and frustrated.

WARNING: Monotasking may lead to extended periods of deep concentration, focus and accomplishment. Uninterrupted work on a single project for a period of time may provide user feelings of euphoria and a heightened sense of purpose. Practitioners of monotasking may experience clarity of thought, project completion and increased satisfaction. Monotasking has been known to reduce stress in users. Monotasking can be addictive.

Monotasking is a great way to rekindle your creativity. Losing yourself in a singular task for a period of time provides you with the opportunity to explore, dig deeper, think vertically and horizontally; going deep and wide, finding the connections between what you're working on and other areas. Whether you are monotasking at work or monotasking for your personal enjoyment, you will find your creativity comes out to play. The time you give yourself to focus on one — and only one — subject will pay dividends in multiple areas. Not just for the moment and the project on which you're focused, but also for the satisfaction and peace you will feel by focusing on just one thing which, in turn, will make you want to monotask even more.

What's not to like about that?

Ideas and Inspiration:

Chapter 5
Go Analog

I've alluded to it in earlier chapters - the need to "go analog".
What am I talking about, you ask? I define "going analog" as
using a pencil and paper for your work. Not all of it, but some
of it. Here's why.

Handwriting is almost becoming a thing of the past; nearly
hovering on the brink of extinction. It seems almost nostalgic
at this point. We are more adept at grabbing our phones or
tablets or laptops and punching out a few words than we are
at grabbing a pencil and paper and writing something.
Yet, despite our expanding use of electronics, pencil sales
continually increase[11] year-on-year at a healthy clip.
Surprising, no?

Handwriting is critical for us on multiple levels.
Connections happen between the hand, the brain, and the
eyes that cannot be replicated any other way. Haptics —
non-verbalcommunication involving the hand — are a
critical part of our development and being.

Think about the process of writing something: your hand
grasps a pencil in such a way that it is capable of making
a mark. You hold the pencil in your dominant hand —
unlike typing, it is a one-handed experience, remember?

Your eyes direct your hand to place the pencil on the paper in a specific location. You have to decide what form the letters will take (call it choosing a font if you will), how large the letters will be, how hard to press the pencil which will determine how dark the writing will be, how much space you will allow between the letters, words and lines, when to move down to the next line of text, when to go to the next piece of paper, etc.

It's actually quite a complicated task. You are much more engaged in the experience than you are when you use a keyboard. You have to consciously make numerous decisions when you write something; decisions that you don't have to make when you type.

Handwriting, by its nature, is a slower, more methodical process. Even if you write quickly, it's doubtful that you write faster than you type. This slower process encourages you to be more thoughtful as you write your ideas. It's harder to erase the written word than it is to backspace over text in a document on your computer. Use a pen instead of a pencil and you're into striking through your mistakes. Not nearly as clean as deleting text on a screen.

This slower process allows you time to think about what you are writing and what comes next. It provides time for you to consider your words carefully. It allows you the opportunity to sketch ideas next to your words. To doodle on the same paper while you're thinking. Make notes in the margin and easily add thoughts to earlier passages. Turn the paper and write in a different direction.

Turn it completely upside down and play with the shape the words are creating. Make as many columns as you wish. Readily flip the paper over and write on the back. Write as large or as small as you like — you and only you control what goes onto the paper. OK, some of this sounds a bit silly, but the point is that you have greater freedom when you write by hand than you do with a machine. You also don't need electricity to recharge your pencil and paper.

Writing by hand is also a five-senses experience. You feel the pencil in your hand and feel the graphite as it leaves its mark on the paper. You visually choose where to place the pencil on the page and watch as the letters form (and see whether they are legible or not!). You can smell the pencil. (A freshly sharpened pencil smells great, doesn't it?) You hear your mind speak the words that you're putting down on paper and you hear the pencil as it makes its marks on the paper. You can even chew on the pencil while you're lost in thought, considering what to write next. Have you ever chewed on your keyboard? I didn't think so. Handwriting engages all of the senses unlike the disembodied clacking of your fingers on a keyboard.

As an aside, a pencil is just about the perfect companion for writing. It's capable of writing in zero gravity — good to know, should that opportunity ever present itself. It can write under water although waterproof paper is a little harder to come by. It also writes when inverted — when you are writing upside down, like on a ceiling or something. There is enough graphite in an average pencil to write a 45,000-word book.

Pretty versatile tool especially considering its basic design hasn't changed much over the past 400 years.

Yes, a keyboard or one of your other devices may be an easier and faster way to put words down, but you're looking for inspiration for how to ignite your creativity, right? It's time to mix things up. Try a pencil and paper. Slow the process down just a little bit. Think. Put your thoughts and ideas down on paper and see what appears. Take your time — you're already monotasking and turning off the devices, right? (And no, that was not a test. Well, OK, it was. How'd you do?)

Take the concept a step further: create an "analog" space where you work. You have a space where your machines are — your computer, tablet, phone. Can you create a space — maybe it's right next to your computer but requires you to slide your chair over to it — where you can write? Or use a clipboard and identify a place to sit that together make up your analog space?

Adding a pencil and paper to the equation of turning off your devices and monotasking gives you the trifecta of creative inspiration. Creating an analog space will serve as a physical reminder of its importance to you. Time, focus and using your hand to capture ideas and inspiration will open up new vistas you could never have expected.

Ideas and Inspiration:
(Here's a good place to put "going analog"
into practice!)

Chapter 6
Actively Engage Your Senses

Ah, the five senses: sight, hearing, smell, touch, and taste. Powerful signals and communicators for us.

What's fascinating is how we generally take them all for granted — until one is lost. On a normal day, we use our senses non-stop, unconsciously, most of the time. Yet each one of them are amazing.

Try actively engaging your senses, one at a time and then together, in pairs or more.

Here are some ideas to get you started:

Pop a piece of really good chocolate into your mouth (and I mean the kind you go into a chocolate shop for and purchase just one piece of deliciousness). Let it sit on your tongue and melt. Savor its complex flavors. Close your eyes and try to identify what ingredients are conspiring to give you such an amazing experience. Consider what the chocolatier had in mind when he or she created this marvelous bite for you.

Another good taste is single malt Scotch. I heard a distiller, when explaining how to taste Scotch properly, suggest that it needed to be chewed. Literally. He also suggested that, as the Scotch had been sitting in a barrel for 15 years, the least you could do is let it sit in your mouth for a minute. The experience of letting Scotch settle in your mouth while it opens up and shares its secrets changes the experience completely.

A simpler exercise is, as you eat your meal, really taste the food. If you're in a restaurant, consider how the flavor profiles were built to make that specific bite taste the way it does. The combination of fat, acidity, and sweetness alongside how the food was prepared to give it that particular texture was deliberate. The chef didn't just grab some meat and vegetables and toss them on the plate to accommodate the daily caloric count necessary for you to live; a significant amount of training and thought went into creating the plate that sits in front of you. Consciously taste the flavor combinations and try to understand and appreciate the experience the chef intended for you. As odd as this sounds, even fast food restaurants have this experience in mind, although we tend to shove the food in our mouths and get on with our day, rather than soaking in the experience.

Continuing with food, as you cook at home, think about adjusting your recipe just a bit and see how it changes the experience of the meal you're serving. Adding a different spice or preparing an element differently or changing how you combine certain vegetables with proteins can significantly shift how a plate tastes — for better or worse!

Pushing yourself to prepare something new is a great way to ignite your creativity. Head to your local grocery and grab a vegetable you've never prepared before — or even one you hated as a child — and see what worlds open up for you.

Visually, I am always amazed — and overwhelmed — when I see a paint chip display at a hardware or household paint store. I get it that the spectrum of color is nearly infinite but seeing the paints and their hues and intensities as they move from absolute white to total black is visually amazing. Just a slight change in the color mix creates another unique color. I also love reading the names of the colors. Who thinks up these names anyway?

An art gallery or museum is an obvious place for visual stimulation. One practice I employ is going to a museum for one thing — either a specific show or a specific section or even a specific period. I love art museums but can overdose after moving from gallery to gallery. I mitigate that by choosing one section / show / period / technique, which allows me to really soak up the art in that section; take a deep dive, if you will, without overwhelming myself.

And don't forget the palette presented us daily on this planet we call home. Sunrise (I miss most of them, actually) and sunset, as the sun comes or goes gives us some amazing colors to start and end our days. Consciously watching how the sky changes does two things: it gives us something to focus on for a few minutes (neither sunrise nor sunset last very long) and it is a visual treat as the sky lightens or darkens with all of the colors that emerge from the atmosphere and clouds. Simply lovely.

Put on a favorite piece of music. Doesn't matter what genre, just something with which you are familiar. Listen with intent to it. Listen how the melody and harmonies are built and what instruments went into creating that specific sound. Consider the musicians and technicians creating the music — what training they had, how they worked to give you that experience. Now do the same thing with a piece of music that is unfamiliar to you. Opening your mind to new music — whatever the source — is a way to expose yourself to the creative possibilities that surround you.

Listen to the cacophony of the city. It's overwhelming and sounds like a wall of noise. Yet, it is comprised of a vast number of individual noises that, in concert, give you that blast. Listen attentively and see how many individual sounds you can identify.

The same is true when you go out into nature. Again, the sounds (or lack of sounds) are built one sound upon another. How many individual sounds can you identify? Can you identify specific species of birds? What are the plants that are rustling in the wind? What does each of them offer to the chorus of noise where you are standing?

We have more nerve endings in the tips of our fingers than we have anywhere else on our body. Think about that for just a moment. Touch is a critical part of how we communicate and how we learn about our world. Watch a small baby reaching and grasping for things. If you think touch is not important to adults, walk into a crystal shop and there will be a sign — at adult eye level — that says, "Do not touch."

My mother sewed as a hobby. I recall as a child wandering with her through aisles of fabric. To this day, I love feeling the texture of fabric. And, unlike when I was a child, the fabric varieties being created today are fantastic! There are so many textures to be enjoyed. Check out your local fabric store and just feel the variety of textures available. Amazing.

Take your shoes off. Right now. What do your feet feel? How does that stimulation make you feel? Eliminating the buffers between the nerve endings in your skin and the world around you is a great way to stimulate your senses. To flip it around, imagine how showering in a raincoat would change that experience. Try to eliminate the barriers that prevent you from feeling life.

A coffee roaster is an olfactory orgy, particularly if they roast several types of beans for different blends. While I understand that different beans and roasts create unique coffee blends, only when they are smelled (and tasted for that matter) side by side can the nuances be fully appreciated.

Clearly, a teashop, with its myriad blends and types of tea, offers a similar experience as you attempt to identify the different herbs that have been combined for that unique aroma and taste.

Markets are a place to challenge your senses, in particular spice markets and souks in the Middle East. One minute, you have cardamom and cumin floating by your nose and a few steps later, you're smacked with the stink of chicken poop. Another step and you're smelling tanned leather. I'm at a loss to describe it properly, but it's really a cacophony of aromas and is to be experienced if you have the opportunity.

Smell is one of the most powerful senses we have. Catching a whiff of perfume will take you back to a special moment in your life. The smell of certain foods will likewise conjure up memories as well as kick your appetite into gear and focus your efforts on sustenance. Smells have both positive and negative associations and they are imprinted on our brains.

Savoring an aroma — say from a glass of wine — is a way to focus your attention on how all the elements that are present in that glass combine to give you that particular experience.

By actively engaging your senses, you gain sensitivity to specific situations and better understand the complex world we live in. By isolating your senses during the engagement, you activate receptors in your body that awaken your imagination and enable you to experience the situation on a completely different level.

When you begin to combine your senses again — in pairs or more — you add to the quilt of the experience. The combination of smell and taste is such a normal part of our lives that we don't necessarily appreciate how they shape our experience. Or sight combined with sound. Or touch and how the physical aspect of it impacts our emotional side.

From a creative perspective, the senses play a huge role in how we approach our projects. Focusing specifically on the senses is a great way to wake up creative energy.

Ideas and Inspiration:

Chapter 7
Go Live

It is so easy these days to go home, lock the door, and just nest. Close off the outside world, turn on the device we prefer, and veg out watching a favorite series, film, sport, or whatever. The entertainment choices we have — and I'm just thinking about audio and video at the moment - are virtually endless. We can stream whatever music we want; we have nearly unlimited access to any and all music ever made. Video and its vast selection is literally what-we-want-to-watch-when-we-want-to-watch-it. With eBooks, we can download most any book we want and read it immediately. Or we can flip through endless pages of social media posts and even combine our viewing or listening or reading with social media, sharing the experience with others virtually. In no time at all, hours have simply passed by while we're curled up on our couch. So easy, so comfortable and so isolated.

On the flip side, taking in a live event of any kind takes some effort but it delivers an entirely different experience. A live event engages so many aspects of what makes us living, breathing beings. Hearing — and seeing — a concert live versus listening to it on earbuds is simply more invigorating. Attending a sporting event has a totally different vibe to it than watching it on TV. Seeing artwork in its original form — the technique and materials used and the size of the original work — gives you a perspective and intimacy you cannot get out of a book, or from a video, or on the screen of your computer.

When you attend something live, you add a one-of-a-kind experience to your life for which there is no playback button. You also share that unique experience with others at that moment. You laugh along with the rest of the audience at a funny line in a stage show. You rise and fall with elation and desperation along with thousands of other spectators at a game. You enthusiastically sing along with the throng when the lead singer points the microphone to the audience.

You are engaged. You are alive. You are *there.*

Yes, it takes effort to leave the comfort of your home. Yes, you think about what to wear when you go out to an event. Yes, you have to plan ahead - maybe weeks or even months if tickets are involved. Yes, weather may be a consideration, as is transportation, a babysitter, seating, queues, etc. Yes, you have to make an effort to go to the event when it's happening and try to get there by a specific time. Yes, it is much easier to stay home and not bother.

But, you want to get inspired, right? You want to awaken the emotions inside of you, right? You want to ignite your personal creativity, right?

A live event only happens once. There is no replay. There is only one way to experience it so you absolutely need to get up and go. Head out and take in something — anything — live. Join your fellow enthusiasts and have that shared experience. Throw yourself into the moment and soak up all of the engagement the opportunity offers. Savor the details and the multi-sensory stimulation presented to you. Roll around in it until it sticks to you and envelops you. Let it consume you.

Think about the affect of experiencing something live in a different way. For example, name a present you received on your last birthday. Got one? Now, name a present you received on your birthday two years ago. Can you name one? Unless it was something spectacular, I'd venture to guess that you had trouble naming a present. Why is this so?

Life's best memories don't come from things: they come from experiences. Think back on a favorite trip you took. When was that? Can you go back even further in your life and name another significant experience? A family trip perhaps? A favorite concert you attended? A memorable sporting event? Your first kiss? Why is it easier to remember experiences you've had than it is to remember things you've received?

It comes down to how these experiences are imprinted on your brain. Things are just things — tools, baubles, stuff. They are a part of your life and may help you get from point A to point B, but they aren't a part of you.

Experiences, on the other hand, become part of what makes you, you. Part of your history. Part of what shapes your attitude and outlook. You were there, in the moment. You were there, engaging all five senses. You felt it with your soul, with your heart. It's a combination of physical, mental, and emotional connection to the experience; it engages every aspect of living. Experiences create the person known as you.

Now, if you regularly attend live programs, chances are you attend many of the same kind of events. Perhaps you're a fan of your college football team and attend every home game. Or you go to every opening at a favorite art gallery. Or never miss a concert by your favorite artist when he or she is on tour. Go you! You are getting out there and absorbing the whole experience. Feels great doesn't it? You look forward to these experiences, right?

How about mixing it up a bit once in a while? Pop into a jazz bar when jazz isn't on your usual playlist. Or attend a sporting event when you would otherwise take in the symphony. Perhaps attend an ethnic festival when you're more likely to take a walk in the woods. Do something that challenges the norm — your norm. Do something that takes you somewhere new or different. Challenge yourself. Add to your experience portfolio; broaden your horizons just a wee bit more.

As long as it's live. Because you are alive. And live only happens once.

Ideas and Inspiration:

Chapter 8
Take a Workshop

Taking a workshop is always a good idea. It helps whether you have something you enjoy doing or especially if you are not overly familiar with the workshop's emphasis.

If you have a passion, hobby or interest, a workshop is an easy way to ignite your creativity and help you advance your craft. It's a chance to take a deeper dive into a subject or develop an aspect of the subject with which you need help or wish to understand better. The opportunity to learn from others in a hands-on environment can provide you a powerful boost.

If you don't have a specific passion, hobby or interest but are curious about something, a workshop is a way to test the waters with little risk and get inspired as well. Whether you take up this new interest as a passion or not is less important than the new ideas the workshop will give you just from attending it.

Think about the elements of a workshop:

First, it's a subject that captures your attention: maybe how to pickle home garden vegetables, how to cut dovetail joints by hand, how to fly fish in Slovenian mountain rivers or how to manipulate photos captured on your mobile phone. Each of these examples has a unique angle on a specific subject that will challenge what you already know — assuming you already know something about the subject, that is! Each of these will take you deeper into the subject than where you were before the workshop.

The workshop is offered by an instructor who is well-versed enough to teach a course on the subject. The instructor has, presumably, enough experience in the subject area to impart his or her wisdom to others. At a minimum, it's a person who wants to share his or her knowledge with others to help them further embrace the subject. Someone who's passionate about the subject and wants to help you appreciate and embrace that passion.

It's a course of study designed to step you through the process and advance your knowledge and skills in that subject area and usually within a specific time commitment. Whether the workshop is a couple of hours in the evening or a weeklong residency, the class is designed to teach you certain aspects of the subject and move you forward. It has a defined start and stop time to impart the wisdom to you. Afterwards, you have enough knowledge to move forward, experiment, and apply the lessons to your own work.

You have workshop colleagues who are as eager to learn something new as you are. People from different walks of life and different stages of their work coming together to learn something new. Again, it's a chance to have a shared experience, most likely with people you haven't met before. A chance to connect with and learn from others who share a common interest.

I've found that meeting fellow enthusiasts and learning from them is at least half of the fun of attending workshops. Learning what they do and how they do it. In my case, I'm thinking about my passion for photography. I don't want to copy what other photographers are doing, however learning about certain materials they use or gaining an understanding about a technique unfamiliar to me has led me to breakthroughs with my own work.

One example: while attending one such photo workshop, I learned about the paper one photographer was printing his images on. I was, up to that point, limited in my thinking about photo paper. At the time, I was fairly new to the world of digital printing and simply had not explored all of the paper possibilities. Because of that conversation, I went on a new tangent when I learned about the vast variety of papers that were available and, as a result, how choosing the perfect paper can affect the viewer's experience with the photograph. The paper he was using wasn't what I'd call normal photo paper; rather it was made of mulberry pulp which gave the paper a slightly soft surface with lovely texture and rendered the photo as a semi-transparent image. Up to that point, I had worked with pretty middle-of-the-road, predictable, high-quality yet unimaginative, photo paper. That one chat opened up a new world to me and changed how I have thought about every photo I have printed since that encounter. While I learned a lot from the workshop itself, however, I learned even more from my conversations with fellow photographers.

The camaraderie that can develop between workshop participants is cool. It is great to connect with others who have a shared interest. Often, you'll find a kindred soul whose attitude and outlook are similar to yours which, again, expands the experience and learning.

Workshops are available in almost every community. Check out the offerings from a college, from community colleges to four-year institutions, an art center or museum, your county extension agent, sports and recreation organizations, trade schools, libraries, churches, ethnic communities, music schools, community or professional theatre — the list is endless. A good search on the web will always net possibilities. You'll be surprised how obscure and specific some workshops are. The good news is that if you're interested in learning more about something, someone is most likely offering a course on it.

A workshop is a great way to expand your mind by learning about what others are doing; a chance for you to learn something new. Every session and every conversation will plant new ideas in your head. New ideas will lead to new explorations on your part — again, sparks of ideas that will ignite your creativity and send you in new directions.

Ideas and Inspiration:

Chapter 9
Get the Tools

BBR, baby! (I'm not sure that will catch on as a phrase but, hey, you gotta try, right?) Buy, Borrow, Rent. Now, before I explain what that means and before we go any further I need to warn you that I will be contradicting myself in this chapter. But it will make sense in the end. At least I hope it will.

A great way to jumpstart your creativity is to get the necessary tools in your hands. Literally. That said — here comes the contradiction — we all love excuses for why we cannot do something. Sounds crazy and counterintuitive, but it is true.

We may not readily admit that we love finding excuses, but we really do. Excuses get us off the hook and help us push the commitment to another time in the future.

We regularly look for reasons to justify our inertia; reasons why something is the way it is or why we haven't started a project or why we aren't doing something, especially if it's something that's even a little self-indulgent.

One excuse, though often not verbalized, is guilt. For some reason we often feel guilty about investing in something that's somewhat selfish, like a creative endeavor. I'm not talking about splurging on some article of clothing or something for your home; I'm talking specifically about something that's more personal than that. Something that, on the surface, may seem extravagant.

I'm not going to do a deep dive on guilt and what to do about it here. I think an entire book is called for to address guilt and creativity, its causes, and potential solutions. In fact, there are already plenty of books out there to help you deal with guilt written by professionals who've studied it as a career. I just touched on it here because it is real, it is a factor, and it may be holding you back. Something to consider.

The excuse I do want to dig into, though, is a personal favorite. It's also a lot less complicated than guilt. Sometimes, the real reason for not doing something is that you lack the tools necessary to create or achieve that particular something. Try to chisel stone with a butter knife — you may make some headway depending on what stone you're carving but, at a minimum, you're not going to get where you ultimately want to go. At least easily.

Try traveling internationally without a passport. Or learning how to play the guitar without a guitar. It's just not going to happen.

One of the best ways to tip the scale, to get the ball rolling, to grease the wheels, to, to, um - you'll be happy to know I've run out of idioms — is to buy the tools. Once you are holding the tool you need in your hand, you have no more excuses. That's an inertia breaker; a nudge in the right direction.

Besides it feels good! Holding that tool in your hand somehow legitimizes the project you want to start. Much like Descartes'[12] famous quote, "I think, therefore I am," if you have clay, you are a ceramicist. Canvas, brushes, and oil paints, a painter. A camera, you are a photographer. You are now in the club.

Having the minimum tools you need to start a project is essential and a great way to ignite your creativity. A great way to get you moving. That key obstacle is now gone! Nothing says "create" like having the tool you need in your hand ready to go.

Here's the next obstacle: what if you can't afford the tool you need? Or can't get exactly the one you want for some reason? What then? Remember: Buy, Borrow, Rent.

Options are available when it comes to getting the tool you need that's necessary to get started. In some cases, borrowing or renting is a low-risk, lower cost way to achieve your goal. Say you want to learn how to play the string bass. Borrowing or renting one significantly lowers the cost threshold holding you back from learning. Or a potter's wheel and kiln — those are big expenditures for an individual wanting to learn the process and they are readily available at community colleges and art centers. A passport, though, is something you have to buy if you want to travel internationally. Once it's in your hand, however, you are that much closer to visiting a foreign land.

One important thought about tools: you don't necessarily need the top of the line tools to get started. Buying a nice camera doesn't make you a better photographer any more than buying a nice pen make you a better writer... I regularly tell my photography students, "If you can't be with the camera you love, love the camera you're with." Leverage what tool you have; embrace it.

If you can't be with the camera you love, Love the camera you're with.

Yes, you need certain tools to accomplish certain tasks, but sometimes not having the perfect tool — the exact model you desire — opens up the possibilities for creativity, forcing you to think outside of the box.

My favorite camera happens to be a plastic children's camera from the 1960s. Understand, aside from using film, the entire camera is plastic. There is no zoom or flash and the settings to change the exposure are minimal. In short, it's pretty much a piece of junk as cameras go. Your mobile phone is infinitely superior to this camera in terms of features and capabilities.

But I love it. Because of its limitations, it frees me up to create unique images I cannot create with my much fancier Nikon. Yes, my digital camera has all of the settings I need and a zoom lens and a preview screen, and adjustable shutter speed and aperture, and a flash, etc. It's a normal digital camera with enough bells and whistles to allow me to capture technically great photos.

But the plastic camera is special. If I were to write a book about it, I'd title it, "Shoot, Pray, Develop". It's a film camera so there is no preview screen. It is back to the dark ages photographically, even in comparison to other film cameras. The range finder (how to "see" what the camera is seeing) is close but it's not exact. As I've learned about this camera - it all comes down to experimenting with it — I've lost dozens of images because of the camera's limitations.

Have I shared enough of its flaws so you understand how inadequate this tool is? All of these flaws aside, if you could see my face as I write this, I'm all misty eyed. I love this camera.

I want to shoot film. I have this camera. I have a tool that works, that enables me to shoot images. Is it a "perfect" film camera? What definition are you using for "perfect"? No, even in comparison to other film cameras it is inferior. But the images it captures are magical and, as tools go, it has enabled me to create unique film images; to achieve what I set out to do. I have grown to love this little plastic wonder because of its flaws.

I bought the tool. It was cheap and obviously wasn't top-of-the-line — and my excuses for trying something new went away.

What is it you want to try? What's holding you back from trying it, really? Go buy, borrow or rent the tools you need to get going. Whatever tools you hold in your hand to create what it is you want to create are great. They may not be perfect, but as long as you have them, you can create. With the tools, the excuses you had are gone and the inspiration that comes with the tools will give you the energy you need to get started.

Ideas and Inspiration:

Chapter 10
Take Time Off

Most everyone gets vacation or holiday time of some kind from their employer. How much time off you get a year is less important than what you do with it.

You do take all of your holiday time every year, right? If not, consider this: no one has ever said as they lay on their deathbed, "I wish I had spent more time in the office..."

A great way to rekindle your creativity is taking time off. I mean *really* taking time off — and none of this answering-a-few-emails-for-an-hour-or-so-each-day-while-you're-sitting-on-a-beautiful-beach-somewhere-warm taking time "off" nonsense either. I mean a clean break away from the daily pressures that allows you to soak up the moment where you are. Just time to think about nothing or at least leave the real world behind for some time so you can gain some perspective on all of it and recharge your personal batteries.

While you may feel that you have to stay in touch with what's going on "back at the ranch," the harsh reality is that the business is moving ahead without you being there and you are replaceable.

If you were suddenly abducted by aliens, business would go on without you. The company and your colleagues / employees / team / board / shareholders / students would adjust and things would move along pretty much the same as before you departed in the spaceship. I'm not saying it wouldn't be difficult for them or take some time for adjustment and recovery from your departure, but as you would be out of the picture unable to assist, they'd find a way to move ahead. Without you. If they can do that while you're speeding off to another planet, can they survive for the few days you are out of touch enjoying some down time? That was a rhetorical question, just so we're clear.

I know all of this sounds harsh. I have never met anyone who tried to do a poor job at his or her work. Everyone wants to make a meaningful contribution to whatever is their chosen field and the company for which they work. Most people take their job seriously, want to feel valued, and want to ensure they're supporting their colleagues or team members while being accountable to key stakeholders. Be secure in the knowledge that your contribution is important, but also recognize that it's not the whole enchilada. We'd all like to think that the place can't run without us, but it can and it will. Companies are essentially machines and are quite capable of, and comfortable with, changing out personnel like gears.

Given that reality check, are you ready to use your time off? Are you ready to give yourself a much needed and deserved break? Are you ready to give yourself permission to relax for just a bit? Let the knots unwind from your shoulders and your mind wander for some time?

Like a good night's sleep, a break from the daily pressures and deadlines is a chance to recharge your personal batteries. A chance to give yourself some perspective on your life by disconnecting for a bit. A chance to challenge your mind in a positive way that's not associated with the daily grind (even if you love your work). A chance to do something — anything — different from what you usually do every single day.

Giving yourself time away is a perfect opportunity to indulge in something you love to do, but never seem to have the time to do it. Like a favorite hobby sitting at home waiting for you to break it out. Or a chance to explore something you've always wanted. Or try something you've never considered doing but now have the opportunity to do so. Or visit someplace that's been on your list.

I don't need to put specific ideas in your head — I know you already have a list going — it's been there for a while, hasn't it? You are just waiting for the right time to dive in. I do have one idea, though, to get you started, since the goal of this book is to spark your creativity.

Here's your assignment: As you're heading out the door from work for your much-needed time off, stop by a good newsstand and grab six magazines that you have never read. Magazines whose subjects are so far away from anything you have ever shown any interest in. Read them. Or at least thumb through them and be exposed to something new for you.

You'll be surprised how something so seemingly unrelated to your world will connect back to the familiar while adding a new dimension to it. How an idea from an unfamiliar subject will spark ideas on something you are familiar with. Or kindle an interest in a new area of some kind. Regardless, these magazines will surprise you and send you in new directions. Trust me on this one.

The important thing is that you are taking much needed and much deserved time away from work. A break from the daily hustle and bustle and pressures of your normal life leaves you free to explore. Free to give your batteries a slow recharge. Free to just ponder and daydream.

Time away can be one of the most fulfilling ways to ignite your creativity. Just taking the time to switch off the normal and engage in the present with no specific agenda will add a new dimension of energy to your life and soul.

Another margarita, anyone?

Ideas and Inspiration:

Chapter 11
Travel Somewhere

One of the best ways to get the most out of the above experiences and really indulge yourself with inspiration is to travel. Preferably somewhere new. Extra points for a place where the native language is not your mother tongue.

I don't know what it is about traveling somewhere new and foreign; maybe it awakens our brainstem "fight or flight" responses? Whatever it is, there is nothing like traveling somewhere for the first time. It is magical. You are alert to every little detail — all five senses are immediately engaged, capturing and recording information to help you get your bearings and gain an understanding of where you are and what you need to do next. You find yourself being drawn to every little movement, reading every sign, recording colors, architecture, faces, designs, textures. As you get settled in, you're registering all of the new aromas (for better or worse!), as well as how everything tastes — in particular the local food and beverage. You are also hearing new things — different languages or accents, local music, television shows, radio broadcasts. Yes, it may be the din of a city but it's *that* city.

"You never forget your first time," is a phrase that's widely used for certain life experiences. It also applies when you first visit somewhere new. Being thrust into a new environment with your senses on full alert is incredibly memorable and stimulating.

TIP: Here's my one tip to help you have the best experience you can in whatever country you visit. If you don't speak the language to any workable degree, at least *try* the language. If you can utter the greetings of the day (good morning, good afternoon, good evening, good night), say, "please" and "thank you", "hello" and "goodbye" and even say, "Do you speak English?" (or whatever your native language is) in *their* language, you are set. Just trying the local language suggests you recognize that they do have their own language and you are a guest in their country. Regardless of their command of your language (or, throughout most of the world, their command of English) you will receive better treatment just because you tried to speak to them in their language.

Extra credit for learning "Two beers, please." This last phrase will serve you well. If you're alone, you'll get two beers. If you're with someone else, you're both covered and if you're with two others, three orders will ensure you all have two beers each. Cheers!

Important phrases

— Please
— Thank you
— Hello
— Goodbye
— Good morning
         afternoon
         evening
         night
— Do you speak (my
        native language)?

— Two beers, please!
— Cheers!

When it comes to traveling, I've heard some folks say that money is an issue, and it may be. Most of the people who say that, have simply made other things a financial priority over travel. Like eating out. Or buying that new article of clothing. Or some other decision for how and where money is spent, so that when it comes time to consider travel, there's not enough left to do so. Like everything, it is a choice.

Some people I visit with are concerned about safety and security. I travel regularly and travel around the world. My two rules are: I don't put myself in dangerous situations and I always take a dose of precaution when I travel.

There are places in every country of the world that should be avoided if you're not from there. Certain parts of a city that are dangerous for outsiders (and sometimes even insiders). It's simple: don't go there! There are plenty of other places that are as safe as anywhere else on this planet to visit and have an amazing experience.

The "dose of precaution" is simply to keep yourself safe as you do most days where you work and live. Just don't leave yourself open for exploitation. This includes not flashing a wad of cash around when you shop or leaving your bags unattended. Common sense kinds of things.

A third tip is to try to blend in with the local crowd just enough to suggest that you are not a tourist. I always observe the locals when I first arrive somewhere and do my best (as well as a tall, white, bald, middle-aged male can!) to blend in. I observe their behavior and try to mimic it; I really don't want to stand out as a tourist.

Those three tips filed away, it's a planet full of amazing sights and lovely people who are happy you chose to come see their corner of the world. There is far more good than evil out there despite what the daily news tells us. In fact, traveling abroad is a great way to learn firsthand about what's true and what's not. As humans, we have more in common than we sometimes think we do. Traveling and learning more about other cultures — whilst in their culture — is one of the best ways to reduce prejudices and misconceptions, an extra benefit beyond sparking your creativity.

New vistas and expanding your portfolio of life experiences will necessarily ignite your creative side. The joy is in the going; embracing the journey and all its ups and downs. Learning how to adapt to the local speed of life. Having your senses stimulated with your brain, heart, and gut registering your myriad reactions to these new stimuli.

Convinced yet? I certainly hope so! What country has always been on your bucket list? What are you waiting for? No, really? Grab your passport, book your flight, embrace the diversity and enjoy the ride. You will return home exhausted, stimulated, and inspired.

P.S. While I wholeheartedly encourage international travel (that was pretty obvious), another travel idea is to visit somewhere close to where you live. Remember "inattentional blindness" from earlier? This applies as well to areas near where we live. Often, traveling involves visiting somewhere far away from home; it's not a trip unless you go somewhere, right? Purposely visiting sights or communities near where you live can open your eyes and inspire you in new ways as well. Plus the cost to do so is virtually zero. One more excuse crossed off the list!

Ideas and Inspiration:

Chapter 12
The ½ Idea

Ah, you're looking for the ½ idea the title promised, aren't you? Admit it, saying I was offering you 11 ½ ideas to spark your creativity was a fairly clever way to get you to buy this book because, if nothing else, your curiosity was increased with the "½" mention, right? What is a ½ idea anyway? On the surface it doesn't really make sense. Well, here is the ½ idea and here's the secret: while it seems illogical, there is such a thing as a half idea.

First, consider the ½ concept. Remember when you were a small child and you were asked how old you were? You weren't six and you weren't yet seven, rather you were six *and a half.* An important distinction, right? You were no longer six and you weren't yet seven years old. You were something special somewhere in between the two.

Or the famous question asking whether your cup is half full or half empty. It's neither full nor is it empty; it, too, is somewhere in between.

So, how does this apply to you and your creativity? How can a creative spark be only half of one? In this case, instead of suggesting to you something significant to try as I did in the previous chapters, how about making a small adjustment to what you are already doing? The concept is to do something slightly more than is expected and do it in a way that is unconventional. Adding a little twist to something that makes it unexpected. Hence, the ½ idea.

Yes, in itself, it could be an entire idea but by positioning it as just half an idea changes how you perceive it. I mean, is a half idea half baked? Incomplete? Does it leave you hanging? Not at all. I think there's more to it than meets the eye.

Here's a way to think about a ½ idea and how to apply it to your situation: What are you working on that could be adjusted a little to make it more interesting? What are you doing that needs just a little more added to it to make it unique? How can you twist something to give it a new look, a new angle, a new perspective?

Take a project you are currently working on — it can be something from your work, something creative you're doing or even something around your home, like organizing your garage. Not completely reworking an idea, or starting over on the idea, but rather giving it a nudge in a new direction. Looking at it differently.

What you want to do here is gain a new perspective on that project. Here are several ways to do that:

Try this for starters: go to where you do most of your work— either your "day job" or where you do your creative things — your studio, workshop, office, kitchen, garage, spare bedroom — wherever you do most of your creating.

Climb up onto your desk / table / counter / bench — you know, the horizontal surface where you do your work. If you don't think that it'll support you, use a stepladder, but set it right next to where you usually work. Climb up there and take a good panoramic look at your workspace. What do you see? Looking at where you create from an unusual vantage point will give you a new perspective on your work. Look critically at the layout below you and consider what could, or should, change in order to give your work that ½ idea nudge.

Does the workflow make sense? Are your machines where they really should be? Can you move around your space in a logical and convenient fashion? Where is the light and can you make better use of it? Do you have a place to "go analog" there? If not, how can you create that space?

What about a refresh of your space? Have anything you can get rid of that is really not important and takes up space? What about adding a new plant? Changing your chair? Turning your desk around in the other direction from where it is today? Painting the walls a new color? Changing the artwork on the walls to make it feel new?

You will find that if you move, change, add or eliminate even just one thing, that one change alone will send you in a new direction. Maybe just slightly — just half way — but it will make a difference.

Another approach is to take your project and turn it upside down or look at it backwards - physically change the perspective and flow of it. Review a process you've developed from the end to the beginning. Turn a design, a presentation, a photograph or a painting upside down and consider the composition from that angle. Literally turn something you are actively engaged in around / backwards / upside down and look at it from that perspective. What ideas does this new perspective give you?

A third idea is to reassess your physical proximity to a project. We are always balancing how close we need to be to a project in order to be effective. Sometimes we need to be at what I call the "whisker level" where we see and are engaged in all of the minute details of the project. Other times, we need to take it all in like a landscape panorama, where we pull back and look at what we're doing from the 30,000-foot level.

Take a project you are working on and shift your perspective. Move closer or farther away based on how close you are to it at this moment.

And, in case it's not clear, these ½ ideas aren't isolated; you can use them in tandem for added impact. Combine them like spices in your pantry and see what happens. A pinch here and a pinch there, so to speak. Change how close you are to a project by turning it upside down. Reorganize your workspace and look at the workflow from the end to the beginning.

What's happening is that you are making a slight adjustment to something you are already doing to see how that tweak changes things. To see if it sparks new ideas. Just a change in angle and/or literal distance is sometimes all that's needed in order to re-see a project and reignite your creativity.

Not a huge change, just, you know, a ½ idea.

Ideas and Inspiration:

Afterword

How is something ignited? What does it take to ignite a flame? Or passion? Or creativity? Most of the time all it takes is one spark. One simple spark placed in the right spot to get things going.

Think about a literal spark. Like when you walk across the room, touch something metal, and get that little shock. Or when you first strike a match. Light a firework (my favorite!). Turn on a gas burner or grill.

How long does that spark last? It is present for only a few milliseconds, hardly any time at all but its impact is amazing. By itself, it is pretty, but inconsequential. A spark is a catalyst — its form remains unchanged while it creates change in other things. It needs fuel to really make something happen.

And what change a spark can create! Its impact — what it ignites — can be tremendous! What gets ignited can explode and/or burn for a long time — forever even — as long as there's fuel to keep it going. A spark without fuel, though, is just that: a spark. A small flash of no real consequence.

We all need that spark ignited for us once in a while. That one thing that ignites something within us.

Each of the 11 ½ ideas shared here are designed to provide that spark for you. To be that millisecond of ignition to help get your creativity burning. Some may require more fuel — extra energy on your part — than others, but that is normal based on your needs, priorities, and possibilities.

If you think about it, the 11 ½ ideas fit nicely into a one-year calendar — one idea per month. To avoid being overwhelmed, try one idea a month and see how each of them work for you, building on one another.

You have 11 ½ ideas to get you going; to mix things up a bit; to ignite your creativity. The reading is over; it's time to get moving. Time to add fuel to the sparks you received.

I genuinely wish you great success as you ignite your creativity! Please let me know how it goes for you. I'd love to hear from you. Please write me at dennis@ DennisHodgesSpeaks.com.

Dennis Hodges believes that everyone is creative. All of his work is focused on helping others get in touch with their creativity, where he serves as a creative catalyst or "creatalyst." He is a fine-art photographer, a strategist and, as may be apparent, passionate about nurturing creativity and creative thinking. This is his first book. He lives in Kansas with his wife, Judit. Dennis presents engaging keynotes and workshops worldwide on creativity and creative thinking. For booking information please contact him at dennis@DennisHodgesSpeaks.com

END NOTES

1. "Ignite", Oxford Living Dictionaries, https://en.oxforddictionaries.com/definition/ignite

2. Nick Perham, "Music only helps you concentrate if you're doing the right kind of task", last modified November 9, 2017, http://theconversation.com/music-only-helps-you-concentrate-if-youre-doing-the-right-kind-of-task-86952

3. "Albert Schweitzer Quotes", Brainy Quote, https://www.brainyquote.com/quotes/albert_schweitzer_402282

4. Christian, Jarrett, "You're most creative when you're at your groggiest", last modified January 18, 2012, https://digest.bps.org.uk/2012/01/18/youre-most-creative-when-youre-at-your-groggiest/

5. "Inattentional blindness", Wikipedia, last modified March 10, 2018, https://en.wikipedia.org/wiki/Inattentional_blindness

6. "Interview with Edward de Bono, author, physician, consultant", The Report Company, last modified June 16, 2014, http://www.the-report.com/reports/malta/open-for-business-and-looking-east/interview-with-edward-de-bono-author-physician-and-consultant/

7. "Hawthorne effect", Wikipedia, last modified March 22, 2018, https://en.wikipedia.org/wiki/Hawthorne_effect

8. Dorota Pawlowska and Monika Dabrowska, "Powerful Pauses", July 27, 2013

9. "Luddite", Wikipedia, last modified April 1, 2018, https://en.wikipedia.org/wiki/Luddite

10. Vivian Giang, "These Are The Long-Term Effects Of Multitasking", Fast Company, March 1, 2016, https://www.fastcompany.com/3057192/these-are-the-long-term-effects-of-multitasking

11. Rani Mola, "Remember Pens and Pencils? They're Doing Just Fine", Wall Street Journal, October 6, 2014 https://blogs.wsj.com/numbers/remember-pens-and-pencils-theyre-doing-just-fine-1830/

12. "Cogito ergo sum", Wikipedia, last modified April 28, 2018 https://en.wikipedia.org/wiki/Cogito_ergo_sum